Foreign Language Framework

for California Public Schools
Kindergarten Through Grade Twelve

Developed by the

Foreign Language Curriculum
Framework and Criteria
Committee

Adopted by the

California State Board of Education

Publishing Information

When the *Foreign Language Framework for California Public Schools: Kindergarten Through Grade Twelve* was adopted by the California State Board of Education on November, 10, 1988, members of the Board were: Francis Laufenberg, President; Jim C. Robinson, Vice-President; Joseph D. Carrabino; Agnes Chan; Perry Dyke; Gloria S. Hom; Maryela Martinez; Marion McDowell; Kenneth L. Peters; David T. Romero; and Armen Sarafian.

The framework was developed by the Foreign Language Curriculum Framework and Criteria Committee. (See pages viii—x for the membership of the full committee and the names of the principal writers and others who made significant contributions to the document.) The framework was edited by Marie McLean, working in cooperation with Tomas Lopez. The document was prepared for photo-offset production by the staff of the Bureau of Publications, California State Department of Education, with cover design by Paul Lee and layout design by Cheryl Shawver McDonald. Typesetting was done by Anna Boyd, Regina Gutierrez, and Leatrice Shimabukuro.

The framework was published by the California State Department of Education, 721 Capitol Mall, Sacramento, CA 94244-2720. It was printed by the Office of State Printing and distributed under the provisions of the Library Distribution Act and *Government Code* Section 11096.

© 1989 by the California State Department of Education

ISBN 0-8011-0804-7

Ordering Information

Copies of the *Foreign Language Framework for California Public Schools, Kindergarten Through Grade Twelve* are available for $5.50 each, plus sales tax for California residents, from the Bureau of Publications, Sales Unit, California State Department of Education, P.O. Box 271, Sacramento, CA 95802-0271 (phone: 916-445-1260).

A list of other publications that are available from the Department may be found on page 46 of this publication.

Contents

State Board's Message

THE *Foreign Language Framework for California Public Schools: Kindergarten Through Grade Twelve* presents a new direction for the teaching of foreign languages. In the framework school districts and schools throughout California are challenged to offer foreign language programs that broaden cultural understanding and foster the social and economic benefits resulting from learning another language. And educators are challenged to help students develop the ability to communicate effectively in at least one language in addition to their native language.

Because the State Board of Education has a constitutional responsibility to adopt instructional materials for students in kindergarten through grade eight, it is our intent that this framework influence the development of materials for a foreign language program that begins as early as possible and extends through grade twelve. In that regard we believe this framework will be useful to those responsible for curriculum planning at the local level for schools and districts.

Our appreciation is extended to the members of the Foreign Language Curriculum Framework and Criteria Committee. They have completed an extraordinary task in a very short time. We express our thanks also to the Curriculum Development and Supplemental Materials Commission, especially the Foreign Language Subject Matter Committee, which is chaired by Carol Sparks.

We must communicate to students, teachers, parents, and the community that the study of foreign languages is not only important and rewarding but also necessary. The State Board of Education wants all students to benefit from a foreign language program that will broaden cultural understanding, strengthen democratic values, and prepare students for living and working in the twenty-first century.

FRANCIS LAUFENBERG, President
JIM C. ROBINSON, Vice-President
JOSEPH D. CARRABINO
AGNES CHAN
PERRY DYKE
GLORIA S. HOM

MARYELA MARTINEZ
MARION McDOWELL
KENNETH L. PETERS
DAVID T. ROMERO
ARMEN SARAFIAN

Foreword

I N THE TWENTIETH CENTURY THE UNITED STATES HAS HAD THE mainstream view that learning a foreign language was something for the academic elite, not the average citizen. That long-standing attitude is, however, rapidly giving way to a new and challenging reality. Simply put, the world has become too small, too interdependent, and too competitive a place—economically, socially, and politically—for the average American to continue to wander through it tongue-tied and uncomprehending.

As a crucial part of the ongoing school reform movement, California and the nation have awakened to the central role that studying a foreign language plays in the education of *all* its students. Because learning another language brings such huge advantages—increased earning power, broadened cultural understanding, and sharpened intellectual skills, for example—every student should have a chance to share in the bounty.

The good news is that enrollment in foreign language classes in the state's public schools increased by nearly one-third between 1981 and 1987. More students in California are studying a greater variety of languages at a higher level of proficiency than ever before. On the other hand we still have a long way to go. Only 14 percent of the state's students in kindergarten through grade twelve were enrolled in language classes other than English in 1988. Fewer than one in five of the students were enrolled in an advanced class. Enrollment in key strategic languages, such as Japanese, Russian, Chinese, and Arabic, remains minuscule.

How can we do better? I enthusiastically endorse the impetus for change mapped out in this *Foreign Language Framework*. The framework is a forward-looking document whose main theme—that foreign language instruction should be communication-based—offers the best hope that significantly larger numbers of students can soon be achieving real mastery of additional languages in California's schools. The framework also identifies other key reform issues: the need to start earlier and dedicate more time to second-language instruction, for example, as well as the need to help students who already speak other languages to continue to develop those skills.

Many school districts are moving steadily in the direction outlined in this document. Those districts that still have some distance to go should establish task forces to find ways of speeding up the process. A seven-year timetable for translating into concrete programs the vision found here in the framework is proposed in Chapter IV.

Some have called the poverty of foreign language instruction in this country a national crisis. But I am reminded that the ancient Chinese symbol for crisis is composed of the characters for *danger* plus *opportunity*. Working together—and carefully weighing the suggestions found in this document—our schools can meet the challenge.

Bill Honig

Superintendent of Public Instruction

Preface

"What is lofty can be said in any language, and what is mean should be said in none." MAIMONIDES

L ANGUAGE IS POWERFUL. IT FORCES PEOPLE TO THINK, TO GROPE for the right words to express their thoughts, feelings, and points of view. Speech is perhaps the most complicated skill we develop. And most educators agree with Ernest Boyer's assertion in *High School: Report on Secondary Education in America* that one of the main goals of schools should be to help all students develop the capacity to think critically and to communicate effectively through a mastery of language.

Having effective communication skills in English has always been necessary for California's students. But knowing other languages helps students prepare for life in California now and in the twenty-first century. California has a population rich in cultural and linguistic diversity. Most of the world's languages are spoken here, and immigrants continue to arrive daily. Students who know other languages will be able to communicate better with all residents of California and understand the many cultures that contribute to California's social and economic communities. In addition, students who know other languages will be better prepared to compete for jobs in California's expanding world markets.

The members of the Foreign Language Curriculum Framework and Criteria Committee realized the social and economic benefits to California of developing students with foreign language skills. Consequently, in this framework they proposed a communication-based program beginning in the early grades and continuing through elementary school and high school. The goal of the program is to develop generations of Californians capable of communicating and of doing commerce in the Western Hemisphere, Asia, and other parts of the world.

Developing generations of Californians skilled in foreign languages is an imposing challenge to all of us concerned about education in California. We in the Department of Education urge administrators and teachers throughout the state to use this framework to develop well-planned, communication-based foreign language programs beginning in the early grades. Working together, we can develop Californians prepared to meet the exciting challenges inherent in California's diverse cultures and increasing world markets.

JAMES R. SMITH
Deputy Superintendent
Curriculum and Instructional
Leadership Branch

TOMAS LOPEZ
Director
Office of Humanities
Curriculum Services

FRANCIE ALEXANDER
Associate Superintendent
Curriculum, Instruction,
and Assessment Division

Acknowledgments

THE *Foreign Language Framework* WAS DEVELOPED BY THE Foreign Language Curriculum Framework and Criteria Committee. The members of this committee represented the best foreign language educators in California. They reviewed and discussed current research in foreign language instruction and anticipated the educational needs of effective citizens in the twenty-first century.

We appreciate the efforts of the committee, whose members worked so diligently. Special thanks are due to the chairperson, Carol Sparks. A list of the members of the committee follows[1]:

Carol Sparks, Committee Chair; Teacher of Spanish, Foothill Middle School, Mt. Diablo Unified School District

Tim Allen, Director, Office of Second Language Acquisition, San Diego Unified School District

E. Elaine Bennett, Teacher of Spanish, Mira Mesa High School, San Diego Unified School District

Tei Dacus, Teacher of Japanese, Alisal High School, Salinas Unified School District

Joann Rubino Enos, Teacher of Spanish/Italian, Montera Junior High School, Oakland Unified School District

Janet Fisher, Instructor, Foreign Languages and ESL Teacher Training, School of Education, California State University, Los Angeles

Sidney Gorman, Coordinator, Foreign Languages Programs, and Teacher of American Sign Language, Fremont Unified School District

Richard Haynie, Coordinator, Foreign Languages/ESL Programs Education Center, Fresno Unified School District

Anne Jensen, Coordinator, Foreign Languages Programs, Campbell Union High School District

Virginia Murillo, Coordinator, Foreign Languages Staff Development Programs, Parkside Center, San Francisco Unified School District

Alternates to the framework committee were the following:

Nancy Bainter, Teacher of French, Alisal High School, Salinas Unified School District

Norman Leonard, Teacher of German and Latin, San Diego High School, San Diego Unified School District

Sandra Scherf, Teacher of Spanish and French, La Jolla High School, San Diego Unified School District

Karl Schneider, Teacher of German, Chino High School, Chino Unified School District

---

[1]Titles of the committee members were current when this document was being prepared.

Three resource consultants to the committee were the following:

Duarte Silva, Director of Foreign Languages, California International Studies Project

Marjorie Tussing, Director, Oral Language Proficiency Project

Hal Wingard, Executive Director, California Foreign Language Teachers Association (CFLTA)

The ideas, concerns, and forward-looking recommendations of the committee were reflected in the framework written by **Gerald Logan.** The final draft of the framework presented to the Curriculum Development and Supplemental Materials Commission and approved by the State Board of Education was prepared by **William Boly.**

Guidance and support in the preparation of the framework and facilitation of the approval process were provided by the Curriculum Development and Supplemental Materials Commission. Members of the commission included:

Carol S. Katzman, Chair; Director of Educational Services, Beverly Hills Unified School District

Dan Chernow, Pacific Theaters Corporation, Los Angeles

Ann Chlebicki, Assistant Superintendent of Instructional Services, Saddleback Valley Unified School District

Mary Ann Church, Superintendent/Principal, Jefferson Elementary School District

Charlotte Crabtree, Graduate School of Education, University of California, Los Angeles

Leroy F. Greene, Senator, State Capitol

William Habermehl, Assistant Superintendent of Educational Services, Office of the Orange County Superintendent of Schools

Dorothy K. Jackson, Assistant Principal, Middleton Street School, Los Angeles Unified School District

Joyce King, Director of Teacher Education, University of Santa Clara

Ernestine Mazzola, Meadow Heights Elementary School, San Mateo City School District

Jack O'Connell, Assemblyman, State Capitol

Fran Smith, Manzanita Elementary School, Conejo Valley Unified School District

Carol Sparks, Foothill Middle School, Mt. Diablo Unified School District

Elizabeth Stage, Director of Mathematics Education, Lawrence Hall of Science, University of California, Berkeley

Thomas Vasta, Teacher/Science Resource Specialist, Elk Grove Unified School District

Elena B. Wong, Associate Superintendent of Educational Services, Stockton City Unified School District

State Department of Education staff members responsible for overseeing the content development of the framework were the following:

Francie Alexander, Associate Superintendent, Curriculum, Instruction, and Assessment Division

Tomas Lopez, Manager, Office of Humanities Curriculum Services

Birgit Bauer, Consultant, Foreign Languages and International Studies Unit

Fred Dobb, Consultant, Foreign Languages and International Studies Unit

Adele Martinez, Consultant and Coordinator of the Foreign Language Framework, Foreign Languages and International Studies Unit

State Department staff members responsible for management of communication and all framework committee activities were the following:

Glen Thomas, Manager, Curriculum Framework and Textbook Development Unit

Jerry Cummings, Consultant, Curriculum Framework and Textbook Development Unit

Members of the Foreign Language Subject Matter Committee of the Curriculum Commission were:

Carol Sparks, Chair and Liaison to the Foreign Language Framework Committee; Foothill Middle School, Mt. Diablo Unified School District

Thomas Vasta, Teacher/Science Resource Specialist, Elk Grove Unified School District

Elena B. Wong, Associate Superintendent of Educational Services, Stockton City Unified School District

Support staff included:

Charlotte Cameron, Commission Secretary
Diane Davis, Language Arts and Foreign Languages Unit
Patti Miller, Office of Humanities Curriculum Services
Gerin Pebbles, Language Arts and Foreign Languages Unit
Dolores Vidales, Office of Humanities Curriculum Services
Linda Vocal, Office of Humanities Curriculum Services

Introduction

In this framework the California State Department of Education has set a challenging goal for California schools. The Department is encouraging all schools throughout the state to develop students who can communicate effectively and with appropriate cultural sensitivity in at least one language in addition to their native language. Reaching that goal is vital if California and the United States are to continue their leadership roles and flourish in the twenty-first century. The *Foreign Language Framework for California Public Schools, Kindergarten Through Grade Twelve* lays out a basic blueprint for developing students who are able to communicate in more than one language.

ABOUT AS OLD AS THE EFFORT TO TEACH FOREIGN LANGUAGES on this planet is the debate over how best to teach them. Over the years one camp has favored teaching language by having students study vocabulary, rules of grammar, and common sentence structures as well as memorize and translate basic passages. Another group has maintained that the best way to teach a second language is to present the skills of speaking, listening, reading, and writing at once—much the way a child picks up the mother tongue—by appealing to the natural human impulse to understand and be understood. In *Twenty-Five Centuries of Language Teaching,* Louis Kelly reports that instruction in a second language has alternated between those poles for the past 2,000 years.

In California this argument has been settled firmly in favor of communicative competence as the major goal for foreign language education. (The term *foreign language* is used here to denote any system of communication that is unfamiliar to students; for example, Russian, Japanese, and German, among others. Most students

In California communicative competence is the major goal for foreign language education.

study a foreign language to communicate socially on straightforward everyday matters. However, helping students feel comfortable in a second language is an ambitious undertaking. Proficiency in a foreign language is not simply a matter of buying bread, milk, and toothpaste and getting repairs carried out on a car. Students must be able to make contact with each other as people, exchange information and opinions, talk about experiences and likes and dislikes, and explore their similarities and differences.

How best can we help students become proficient in a foreign language? Research has consistently indicated that the most effective way to ensure that students can both employ and enjoy the target language is through a communication-based program. A program that is communication-based is one in which the target language is used to exchange meaningful information in the classroom. Such a program helps students develop proficiency in another language by hearing and speaking the language and using the language to read and write about ideas that matter to them.

As desirable as such an approach is, the obstacles to its widespread acceptance are formidable. For example, the writers of most foreign language textbooks still follow a grammar-based format. And since textbooks are frequently used by teachers to plan classroom activities, their use can help to undermine a school district's stated commitment to a communication-based language program. In addition, a grammar-based program may be more convenient for the teacher to manage than a communication-based program, especially in a large class setting. And some teachers trained in the old method of instruction may not clearly understand the difference between the two programs.

In addition to the question of how a foreign language is taught, but also bearing on the goal of achieving proficiency, is the issue of how much time is spent studying a foreign language. No matter how good the pedagogy, students will not become fluent in a second language by attending a 50-minute class five times a week during a single school year. Mastery of a foreign language takes time. (In Europe, Japan, and the Soviet Union, for example, five to seven years generally are allocated to the study of English or another foreign language.) For school administrators interested in building a successful language program, the requirement for a large block of time has two clear implications: First, it signals the need to move the beginning of the serious study of language into the kindergarten through grade eight years. And, second, it highlights the importance of districtwide strategic planning so that continuity of learning is not interrupted. (Appendix A includes information school administrators can use in planning effective foreign language programs.)

The rewards of a well-run, communication-based foreign language program are great in terms of student achievement and satisfaction. But the demands are also considerable: creative and skilled teachers and the support of school counselors and administrators, parents, and other members of the community. The best efforts of thousands of individuals will be required to make the foreign language programs in California's schools what they should be—a means by which far greater numbers of students attain proficiency in a variety of languages. That effort will be forthcoming if people are convinced of the worthiness of the goal. For that reason the framework begins with a review of the most fundamental question of all: Why is there renewed emphasis on teaching foreign languages?

I. Benefits of a Foreign Language Program

The study of foreign languages benefits California and its students by:

- Preparing them to compete and cooperate in the international arena (economic benefits)
- Promoting multicultural understanding (civic and cultural benefits)
- Building intellectual achievement (intellectual benefits)

WHY SHOULD SCHOOLS TEACH FOREIGN LANGUAGES? Why has the ability to communicate in another language long been regarded as an essential element of a well-rounded education? What benefits could a speaker of English, who is a member of the second largest speech community in the world, gain from studying another language?

Ask any multilingual individual those questions and you are likely to be greeted with a few seconds of silence before hearing an answer. There are many reasons to learn a foreign language—as many as the people who speak it. Language is a means of contact with other human beings. However, the educational rationale for studying a foreign language can be divided into three main categories of benefits: economic, civic and cultural, and intellectual.

The educational rationale for studying a foreign language can be divided into three main categories of benefits: economic, civic and cultural, and intellectual.

Economic Benefits

On a pragmatic level, schools in California as well as in other states need to develop more individuals with strong skills in a second language as a matter of long-range economic self-interest. For example, the United States is developing economic and social ties to the Soviet Union. Yet the development of our relationship with the Soviet Union could be curtailed because of a lack of qualified

American-born speakers of Russian. In fact, there are more teachers of English in the Soviet Union than there are students of Russian in the United States.

Also, two-thirds of the translating jobs at the U.S. Department of State are filled by foreign-born individuals because properly trained American-born candidates are not available. In addition, the world has changed since World War II. The language of business is no longer exclusively English; rather, it is the language of the customer and, too often, our sales representatives do not speak the same language. For example, Pepsi Cola's marketing plan for Southeast Asia did not succeed because when translated into Thai its "Come Alive" slogan read, "It raises your ancestors from the dead."

What is true about our nation's need for speakers of other languages is also true for California. California, situated on the West Coast, is a natural gateway for trade with the countries of the Pacific Rim. Two reports on California's economic future, sponsored by the executive and legislative branches of government, included the same recommendation—that schools provide additional instruction in foreign languages.[1]

Civic and Cultural Benefits

A less obvious but equally compelling reason to promote the study of foreign languages is the power language has to foster improved understanding between peoples of various cultural backgrounds. Culture is embedded in language. The Department's goal for developing students who can communicate effectively in at least one foreign language includes "appropriate cultural sensitivity" as a quality to be nurtured in foreign language classes. For example, a student of Japanese might learn that a request from an associate in Japan is rarely refused point-blank but that various cues communicate a polite *no*. A student of Arabic might come to understand that the terms for *host* and *guest* imply more social obligations in the Middle East than they do in the United States.

However, every student of foreign languages eventually discovers that cultural conventions differ from society to society. Some cultural conventions reflect genuine differences in the hierarchy of values, while others simply conceal a deeper human commonality that transcends place and time. This "cosmopolitanizing" function of studying a foreign language is valuable to a country such as the United States, which was founded on the belief that out of many traditions one nation could be established (*e pluribus unum*). And the study of foreign languages is especially valuable in California, where a rich diversity of cultural traditions is represented and where one out of four immigrants to the United States eventually settles.

The study of foreign languages is especially valuable in California, where a rich diversity of cultural traditions is represented and where one out of four immigrants to the United States eventually settles.

---

[1]See *California 2000: A People in Transition.* Sacramento: Assembly Office of Research, 1986; and *Educating Americans for Tomorrow's World: State Initiatives in International Education.* Richmond, Va.: National Governors' Association, 1987.

Intellectual Benefits

The third benefit of studying another language is its salutary effect on students' intellectual development. Obviously, students with skills in a foreign language gain direct access to the literature of the language, with all the mental stimulus the acquisition implies. In addition, poets and writers have long contended that knowledge of a foreign language helps speakers better understand their native language in a way that studying the native language directly never could. That is, to students their native language is transparent and unremarkable. Only when they step outside the all-enveloping medium of language and begin to experience a second language's idiosyncracies do the nuances and texture of their own language become obvious. In addition, insights gained by students in a foreign language class are transferable across the curriculum. For example, analysis of recent scores on *Scholastic Aptitude Tests (SATs)* suggests that the study of a foreign language for one or two years (in grades four to six) will result in improved scores in standardized tests of proficiency in one's native language.

In summary, for students, learning a new language can be an asset in the job market, a spur to personal and intellectual growth, a source of increased self-esteem, and an enjoyable experience. For California and the nation, developing more people with advanced skills in a second language results in many economic, civic, and cultural benefits. Clearly, the benefits justify the investment. How to go about the task of developing and implementing an effective foreign language program is the focus of the next five chapters of this framework.

II. Characteristics of an Effective Program

An effective foreign language program is characterized by:

- Teaching and learning *in* the language rather than *about* the language (communication-based instruction)
- Studying language in its cultural context

Communication-Based Instruction

AN EFFECTIVE FOREIGN LANGUAGE PROGRAM IS ONE THAT IS communication-based. Communication-based instruction is that kind of teaching that helps students to develop the skills necessary to produce and receive understandable messages. In a communication-based language program, teachers focus attention on providing information or content and on helping students comprehend and react appropriately to oral and written messages. Communication-based language programs are appropriate for all age levels and for all levels of language competency—whether the students are first graders responding physically to simple instructions, third or sixth graders learning geography concepts in a second language, ninth graders keeping a diary in another language, or advanced students reading works chosen from the literature of the target culture. In a communication-based program, the emphasis is on an authentic exchange of meaning in the foreign language. Most class time is used to engage in or practice communicating.

In communication-based instruction the language of instruction is the language being learned. Classroom business and procedures are also conducted in the target language. Students soon realize that exchanging information, requests, and commands and discussing feelings, social conventions, and so forth done in another language are similarly done in their own language. The classroom is viewed as

Communication-based language programs are appropriate for all age levels and for all levels of language competency.

7

Part of learning a new language is learning to recognize differences in world views, customs, beliefs, and social conventions.

representing a real community where interchanges about significant issues and ideas occur in the target language.

Students are encouraged to express themselves in the language even though mistakes may be made during initial attempts. Experimentation is a natural part of language acquisition. The teacher's role during such moments is that of a patient coach, modeling and guiding positively, as necessary. Constant correction is detrimental, especially when the mistakes do not interfere with students getting their point across clearly. Students must be encouraged to use the language, and encouraging students is accomplished most effectively in a nonthreatening, supportive classroom.

During intermediate and more advanced instruction, grammar instruction and analysis may be helpful to certain students. However, it is not advisable for students to study the structure of language to learn to communicate, especially in the earlier stages of instruction.

The communication-based instructional program is designed to correspond with the way in which young people acquire language at home. Development of receptive skills (listening and reading) should precede language production practice (speaking and writing) in an alternating or cyclical pattern. In a communication-based instructional program, students constantly extend themselves beyond their most effective proficiency range to higher levels of expression and learn and advance in incremental steps.

Language in Its Cultural Context

A foreign language should be taught as the expression of the culture in which the language is spoken. Knowledge of a society's culture is learned through the use of language. Students who equate target-language expressions with their English-language equivalents often acquire erroneous concepts. Part of learning a new language is learning to recognize differences in world views, customs, beliefs, and social conventions. If a speaker wants to express a certain emotion in a target language—a sense of urgency, anger, impatience, deference, or authority, for example—in what manner can the emotion be expressed? Which voice modulations, facial expressions, and gestures would be culturally appropriate? Students need to learn that cultures are often quite different but that they all have values. The language cannot be separated from the culture that gives it life.

III. Languages Taught in an Effective Program

A model curriculum for foreign languages includes instruction in:

- Commonly taught European languages
- Languages used in the Pacific Rim countries
- English as a second language
- Classical languages
- Native languages for those who speak languages other than English
- American Sign Language

European Languages

ADEQUATE FOREIGN LANGUAGE PROGRAMS INCLUDE instruction in one or more of the commonly taught European languages. French, German, and Spanish are the foundation of foreign language programs in California's public schools. Those languages serve as vital links to our European cultural heritage. They are branches of the same Indo-European language family as English and are used widely in world trade and commerce.

French speakers number over 100 million worldwide. Many Russians speak German, the language in which much literature in scientific research was written. Spanish is the official language of 18 nations in the Western Hemisphere. In addition, 4.5 million Californians speak Spanish. According to the U.S. Department of Labor, an ability to speak Spanish is the foreign language ability most in demand in today's job market.

French, German, and Spanish are the foundation of foreign language programs in California's public schools.

Languages of the Pacific Rim Countries

A progressive foreign language program includes critical languages from the Pacific Rim countries. The importance to Californians of the countries in the Pacific Rim is rapidly increasing. *Looking to California's Pacific Neighborhood,* a report to the Governor and the Legislature by the California Postsecondary Education Commission stresses the critical shortage of students studying Chinese, Japanese, and other languages and cultures.

English as a Second Language

Effective instruction in English as a second language is an integral part of the overall language curriculum in every school with students whose primary language is other than English and who have been identified as limited-English-proficient students. An increasing number of public school students in California are from homes in which languages other than English predominate. About 13 percent of the students enrolled in California's public schools were classified as limited-English proficient (LEP) in 1985. Three-fourths of those students spoke Spanish. Those students have an urgent need to develop a command of English.

In the beginning stages of instruction, strategies for teaching English as a second language resemble those used to teach foreign languages. Both strategies are similar in that they are organized around the goals of communicative proficiency and cultural understanding and a commitment to teaching and learning through the target language. In addition, in both strategies an early emphasis on using language for survival and basic living is viewed as a method of developing more sophisticated communication skills.

Still, significant differences in the strategies exist. For nonnative speakers the "one language in addition to their native language" identified as a goal for foreign language instruction by the Foreign Language Curriculum Framework and Criteria Committee is, of necessity, English, the language of the country in which nonnative speakers now reside. The students receiving instruction in English as a second language have special characteristics and needs, which often differ greatly from those of native speakers of English learning a foreign language. Teachers of English as a second language must have specialized training and instructional skills in addition to those needed by teachers of other languages.

Practically all concepts presented in this framework apply to instruction in English as a second language as well as to instruction in foreign languages. However, instruction in English as a second language has certain dimensions not commonly emphasized in instruction in a foreign language. Those unique features need to be pointed out and planned for. Toward that end basic characteristics of instruction in English as a second language are examined in Chapter VI of the framework.

Classical Languages

Classical languages constitute an important option for many students who are choosing another language to learn. Latin and ancient

Effective instruction in English as a second language is an integral part of the overall language curriculum in every school with students whose primary language is other than English.

Greek are vital parts of many foreign language programs. The canon of works by Greek and Roman philosophers, poets, and historians helps to acquaint students with our society's intellectual and literary roots. Learning classical languages involves the same skills as learning modern languages, but the prioritizing of skills differs markedly. Reading becomes the primary objective, supported by limited skills in listening, speaking, and writing. Grammar as an aid to better communication is focused on frequently.

Latin, especially, provides a useful base for learning how many European languages work. Approximately 70 percent of the vocabulary of formal English and 90 percent of the vocabulary of Spanish are based on Latin. Students increase their vocabulary in a systematic manner through building words and studying the derivation of words, common prefixes and suffixes, and word building. In addition, many students who study a classical language are studying to become proficient in one of the modern languages. Such students develop a powerful array of communicative competencies and access to information and ideas.

Native Languages

Continuing instruction in native languages is offered for those students who already speak a language other than English. Languages that help to strengthen the heritage of individuals and community members in California merit consideration as part of the foreign language curriculum. Classes in Chinese, Spanish, and Vietnamese for students who are native speakers of those languages should be made available. It is crucial for such students to develop proficiency in English, but it is also beneficial for them to continue to develop skills in their native language.

A brief look at the radical change in California's population underlines the need for classes in the students' native languages. In 1974 three out of four students in California's public schools were native speakers of English. By the year 2000, however, students now identified as minority students are expected to make up 75 percent of the student population—a majority by anyone's count and a complete reversal of the old demographic profile. Many students will be those who know to varying degrees both English and a native language.

Unfortunately, students who know both English and a native language are not being served well by foreign language courses. For example, an English-dominant Hispanic who has well-developed oral language skills but underdeveloped literacy skills in Spanish is not going to benefit greatly from an introductory Spanish course. That category of student would profit from a native-language development course in several ways.

First, such a course would focus its efforts where they were likely to do the most good—by helping students make the transition from a colloquial to more formal command of the language. Second, students' self-esteem is often raised when they are given a chance to

Languages that help to strengthen the heritage of individuals and community members in California merit consideration as part of the foreign language curriculum.

increase their competency in a language spoken at home (and when they realize that competency is valued by a respected educational institution). Third, the disproportionately high dropout rate among students from various language-minority groups would be reduced.

Fourth, native-language development classes satisfy the two-year foreign language entrance requirement for the California State University system, thus opening the door to advancement to college. Finally, by building on skills that native language speakers bring to the classroom, native-language development courses have the potential for rapidly becoming prototypical advanced language classes—models for the high level of communication proficiency to which the entire foreign language program can aspire.

American Sign Language

American Sign Language is an option for students choosing to study a second language. Linguists have recently recognized American Sign Language as a language in its own right. It is a rule-governed language with the system and scope of any oral language; and it has its own complex phonology, morphology, syntax, and structure of discourse.

American Sign Language is an option for students choosing to study a second language.

American Sign Language is the language of several hundred thousand deaf people in the United States, including over 5,000 students in California's public schools. The number of schools offering classes in American Sign Language is increasing. Students without a hearing impairment may enroll in those classes. When they do, the state's hearing-impaired students become less isolated from the social and economic mainstream. Their confidence and self-esteem increase. Meanwhile, students without a hearing impairment gain a valuable skill, learn general lessons about the nature of language as a tool of communication, and have their curiosity piqued about learning additional languages.

The major objectives of instruction in American Sign Language resemble those of any language: to enable students to communicate fluently in the target language and become aware of all aspects of the culture of the people whose language they are studying. However, there are several special considerations. Experience has shown that class size is a factor in learning American Sign Language because of the visual monitoring the teacher must do. Video equipment, while not absolutely necessary, is a valuable learning tool.

A one-year course in American Sign Language taken by students while in grades nine through twelve satisfies the graduation requirement of a one-year course in visual or performing arts or a foreign language. However, it is important to note that colleges in California have not yet revised their undergraduate entrance requirements to accept credit in sign language as an equivalent for credit in a foreign language.

IV. Characteristics of a Well-Planned Program

An effective foreign language program exhibits sound planning and coordination, which is represented by:

- A time line for reviewing, planning, and implementing curriculum improvement (a three-phase planning process)
- Appropriate instructional approaches *in* the classroom
- Learning experiences *beyond* the classroom

SUCCESSFUL NEW OR REVISED FOREIGN LANGUAGE PROGRAMS do not just happen. The components of the program need to be clearly stated in writing to ensure that the students' learning experiences in the new language reinforce and amplify each other in coordinated sequences from kindergarten through grade twelve. Any strategy for curriculum improvement, however, must be based on the premise that it is neither advisable nor realistic to attempt to revise a foreign language program quickly. Curriculum improvement, like learning language itself, takes time and draws on finite resources at the district and site levels. For such efforts to be effective, they must be planned and implemented over a reasonable period of time.

Curriculum improvement, like learning language itself, takes time and draws on finite resources at the district and site levels.

Three-Phase Planning Process

The State Department of Education recommends that school districts follow a three-phase process in instituting curriculum changes: (1) assessing the program; (2) planning improvements; and (3) implementing improvements in successive stages. In doing so, districts should consider synchronizing their improvement efforts with the state's seven-year planning cycle in foreign languages. Under such a scheme the 1988-89 school year, the year in which this framework is being released, marks the beginning of a new cycle. School districts should use this framework to begin assessing their current programs.

Briefly, in year two of the cycle, school districts should plan improvements to their foreign language programs. In year three the implementation phase, including pilot programs in a few schools, should begin; and new instructional materials should be selected. In years four, five, six, and seven, the implementation process should continue, subject to review and modification as required.

The state is scheduled to adopt in 1990–91 foreign language textbooks that meet its selection criteria. If possible, school districts should align their foreign language improvement process with the state's framework and textbook adoption cycle. By doing so, they will be in an excellent position to take advantage of the services being offered by the State Department of Education and various supporting institutions. More important, in using the newly published framework as the basis for review and design of improvements in curriculum and instruction, districts will be developing a foreign language program that reflects the most current research in the field.

A short recapitulation of relevant issues for each of the three phases of the seven-year curriculum improvement cycle is included in the following paragraphs.

PHASE 1

Reviewing the Curriculum. During this phase the content and instructional strategies of the districtwide foreign language curriculum are reviewed and compared with the corresponding areas in the framework, and the strengths and weaknesses of the present curriculum are identified. This is primarily a time for collecting information: How many students are studying foreign languages? What level of proficiency are they attaining? Are students starting early enough? How does the variety of language offerings correlate with demographic trends in the district? In addition to gathering numerical data, however, decision makers need feedback from teachers, students, parents, and members of the community about how they perceive the foreign language program and what they want from it. The focus, in other words, is not only on determining what is but also determining what should be.

An important consideration is the degree to which the foreign language program is meeting the needs of each group of students: the gifted and talented, the limited-English proficient, average students, those at risk of dropping out of school, and so forth. In this regard the crucial niches filled by courses in English as a second language and native language development have been described previously. Ordinarily, the best guarantee of curriculum success with the main cross section of students is using a communication-based instructional approach in a vigorous presentation of the target language. In addition, excellent language programs offer a variety of classes calculated to spark an interest in and meet the particular needs and goals

14

of various groups of students. Examples of some frequently employed or particularly imaginative special approaches include:

1. Advanced placement classes at appropriate levels.
2. Immersion-type programs in which some or all of the regular school subjects are taught in a foreign language.
3. Reading classes for more advanced students who plan to do research in the foreign language.
4. Foreign language instruction for students with specialized interests such as business, health care, science, fine arts, agriculture, and so forth.
5. Content-enriched foreign language instruction in which certain topics being studied in other subjects are also the focus in the foreign language class.
6. Exploratory programs in the elementary grades in which mini-courses in several languages are offered. The courses, of short duration, are designed to interest students in the long-term study of additional languages.
7. International language-study programs in which students achieve proficiency in at least two additional languages and take a coordinated schedule of classes in world history and world literature.

> *Success in a communication-based foreign language program is confirmed by what students can actually do with the language.*

PHASE 2

Planning Improvements. During the second phase of the seven-year cycle, a plan for districtwide foreign language curriculum improvement is developed. The plan is based on the findings and conclusions of the first phase assessment. Target languages are selected; and the goals, instructional objectives, and descriptions of the required core content of each course are written. Evaluation procedures and guidelines for placing students in courses are determined, and a plan for staff development is laid out. Instructional materials based on established criteria are adopted, and the revised curriculum is field-tested in pilot classes.

The basic document designed to spell out all of these decisions and ensure uniform objectives and mission is the curriculum guide. Success in a communication-based foreign language program is confirmed by what students can actually do with the language. For that reason the objectives of teaching/learning in a curriculum guide should be stated in specific behavioral terms. For example, a major long-range objective might be that in survival situations students be able to conduct themselves appropriately in the target language. Restated as a series of functional objectives for a particular class level, the expectations might be that students should be able to ask for and understand directions to places in a city or, without offending native speakers, get them to talk more simply or slowly. The teacher is responsible for deciding how behavioral objectives are to be reached during a class period or short lesson.

In terms of course content, curriculum designers must decide which of many possible communicative situations, settings, and topics their students should be prepared for and what students should be able to do with the target language in that context. Those decisions determine much of the vocabulary that students need to acquire.

Next, those language expressions and communicative operations need to be arranged in a priority listing. For example, objectives involving language production (speaking or writing) are normally practiced after mastering objectives designed for comprehension. In addition, threshold or social functional levels have been developed in the target language. Those levels are organized according to the skills and vocabulary students must possess if they are to function effectively in countries in which the target language is spoken.

Planners can also use the general sequence of learning included in the *Model Curriculum Standards,* the *American Council on the Teaching of Foreign Languages Proficiency Guidelines,* the postsecondary *Statement on Competencies in Languages Other Than English Expected of Entering Freshmen,* or other similar manuals (see Selected References). Most sequences suggested in the manuals are quite similar. Alternatively, the local language staff can develop workable guides based on the order in which the language components appear in a communication-oriented language textbook. It is important that a guide be established so that everyone involved is moving in the same direction with a minimum of backtracking.

In designing the new curriculum and bringing it to life, planners and teachers must always remember that encouraging communicative proficiency is essential. If major objectives in a language course are limited, students might satisfy them by mastering a few vocabulary items and language functions such as requesting, identifying, confirming, or thanking. But the overarching goal of communicative proficiency means more than mastering a few vocabulary words. Students who advance beyond the beginning stages of proficiency are able to communicate effectively in unfamiliar situations. Those higher proficiency skills must be developed before students experience the most satisfying dimensions of knowing another language—communicating effectively with speakers of other languages.

Important considerations in selecting foreign language textbooks—another key task in phase two—are included in Chapter VII, Criteria for Evaluating Instructional Materials.

PHASE 3

Implementing Improvements. During the third phase all schools in the district begin using the revised foreign language curriculum. Implementing, monitoring, and modifying the curriculum continue until a new framework is published and the cycle starts over again. The installation of the new curriculum should be supported by an ongoing staff development plan as well as other essential school policy components described in Chapter V of this document.

In designing the new curriculum and bringing it to life, planners and teachers must always remember that encouraging communicative proficiency is essential.

Classroom Instructional Approaches

As previously noted, the teacher bears the challenge of deciding how the functional objectives specified in the district's planning document are achieved in the classroom. Teaching approaches tend to be personal. More than any other component of the instructional process, approaches to teaching reflect the individual characteristics of teachers and students. Individual approaches to teaching are acceptable as long as the curriculum goals and objectives are being met effectively. Developing a suitable approach to instruction is a continuing process for each teacher. Critical factors to be considered in developing a suitable approach include:

1. A method compatible with a goal of communicative competency
2. Classroom organization that facilitates reaching communicative objectives
3. An instructional sequence that reflects the natural process of becoming proficient in using a language well

Teachers should organize the instructional process to promote maximum learning effectiveness. The planning problem is twofold: (1) How can the teacher best organize a learning unit leading to a specific objective? and (2) How can the teacher best organize a class period?

A learning unit includes all those activities that must be done before students can demonstrate their attainment of a specific objective, such as being able to meet a new person appropriately and find out certain personal information about this person. Such a unit may last for a number of days or class periods.

An effective and quite common unit arrangement includes:

1. Introduction of the topic designed to motivate students
2. A presentation or input of new material
3. Guided practice of new material
4. Application of the new material in useful and realistic situations
5. Evaluation

In language instruction the presentation stage commonly consists of oral, visual, or written input done in a variety of contexts and ways until it is comprehended and has become quite familiar. The practice stage consists of controlled exercises designed to help students produce the new elements of the language in realistic contexts. Students might react or respond to commands or questions, give each other cued commands, or ask questions as directed.

The application stage consists of students using the language, most often in pairs or small groups. Students engage in role-playing or problem-solving activities, information-seeking tasks, reporting, describing, telling, writing, playing games, and so forth. Evaluation takes place constantly as the teacher gets feedback during the activities; but a formal evaluation designed to gauge the students' ability to use the target language within the limits of what they have practiced and applied is conducted at the end of the unit.

Individual approaches to teaching are acceptable as long as the curriculum goals and objectives are being met effectively.

A class period is best made up of a variety of activities and tasks. (See Appendix B for examples of communication-based activities.) A single type of activity carried on for an entire period tends to result in less overall learning. Therefore, it is better not to proceed unwaveringly through a single lesson or unit sequence such as that described previously. For example, one class period might include several short tasks involving activities such as:

1. Working on the input phase of a new unit
2. Working on the practice stage of a previously introduced unit
3. Discussing a reading assignment given as homework
4. Presenting or practicing a cultural feature
5. Practicing conversations in small groups
6. Preparing for a writing assignment as homework

By participating in the activities previously listed, members of the class are working toward several objectives during the class period but are at different stages of the learning sequence for each objective. The main point is to provide variety and a change of pace and frequently to renew students' interest and attention.

The final learning task might include unrehearsed demonstrations designed for students to show that they can use the target language to find out personal information from a new acquaintance. Such tasks might consist of simulations, role playing, briefly cued conversations, problem-solving situations, and so forth. The teacher ensures that overall proficiency in using the language is continually being developed in an expanding and integrated manner. Overall proficiency is developed constantly by recycling previously learned material and skills and integrating their use in current communication activities involving more advanced proficiency levels. (See Appendix C for information about proficiency or competency levels.)

Learning Outside the Classroom

Every opportunity to learn foreign languages outside the classroom should be seized eagerly. The limiting factor in developing as high a degree of competency as possible is the scarcity of time. Except in immersion-type classes, the amount of time spent studying foreign languages in school is quite brief. Motivated teachers and students find many cost-effective ways to expand this time.

Beneficial activities involving foreign languages outside the classroom include:

1. Weekend language camps
2. Language fairs and festivals
3. Contests of various kinds
4. Homestays with native speakers
5. Exchange-student programs
6. Study or work abroad
7. Pen pal, audiotape pal, or videotape pal exchanges
8. Field trips

Every opportunity to learn foreign languages outside the classroom should be seized eagerly.

9. Internships in appropriate local businesses
10. Work experience in businesses catering to certain native speakers
11. Hookups to other students in the United States or abroad through the use of shortwave radios, computers, or videos
12. A "sister" class abroad for exchanging many kinds of audio and visual recordings, realia, books, and so forth
13. Foreign language lunch tables at school

V. The Role of
the School

An effective foreign language program is characterized by:

- Essential school policy components, especially:
    1. An articulated sequence for students in kindergarten through grade twelve
    2. Staff development programs for teachers
    3. Integration with other areas of the curriculum
    4. Communication-oriented evaluations
- Appropriate instructional resources, including:
    1. Technology and media aids
    2. Realia and printed materials
- Broad support from:
    1. Schools and districts
    2. Business and industry
    3. Local communities

Essential Components of School Policy

AN EFFECTIVE FOREIGN LANGUAGE PROGRAM OPERATES with certain essential school-based components in place, including an articulated sequence for students in kindergarten through grade twelve, staff development programs, integration with other areas of the curriculum, and communication-oriented evaluations. A description of each component follows.

Articulated Sequence

Students should begin learning a foreign language in kindergarten, and their education should continue in a well-articulated manner through grade twelve.

Students should begin learning a foreign language in kindergarten, and their education should continue in a well-articulated manner through grade twelve. School systems with foreign language programs that span only several grade levels should plan to extend their

20

programs to include all grade levels. It is often advisable to "grow" a program downward. For instance, if the program includes grades seven through twelve, the program may be expanded by adding grades six, five, four, three, two, one, and kindergarten (in that order). That procedure helps to ensure an articulated program without undesirable breaks in the learning sequence for students in kindergarten through grade twelve.

In localities where school districts are not unified, teachers can meet and coordinate language programs to ensure an articulated program for students in kindergarten through grade twelve. Program expansion or extensions should be carefully planned, and teachers at all levels should be qualified. An articulated language program means more than simply making language instruction available in a sequence of grade levels. An articulated language program means having a progression of defined proficiency tasks that students are expected to meet. Articulation is likely to be complicated by the fact that many students enter the beginning proficiency level at various points along the kindergarten through grade twelve grade-level sequence. Articulated programs help to ensure that students are placed at the appropriate grade level.

Staff Development Programs

Teachers assigned to teach languages should be competent in the languages they are teaching. To teach a foreign language, teachers must be able to function at a level equivalent to at least the advanced level on the *American Council on the Teaching of Foreign Languages Proficiency Scale* or at stage three of the California higher education system's *Statement on Competencies in Languages Other Than English Expected of Entering Freshmen* (see Selected Resources). They must also be able to teach toward communicative objectives. If teachers who do not meet minimum standards are assigned to teach foreign language classes, the school district bears the responsibility for bringing teachers up to standard or reassigning them.

The language staff is responsible for identifying those who need in-service staff development and for identifying the type of training needed. Members of the staff should seek opportunities for updating teaching skills and renewing language competency. Languages and cultures are dynamic, and even well-qualified teachers need to frequently renew their skills. Financial support for staff development can come from the teachers themselves, from the school district, or from governmental and private agencies, foreign and domestic.

Novice and veteran teachers benefit professionally from many kinds of experiences, including:

1. Visiting classes of other successful teachers and sharing expertise
2. Using the services of successful teachers in staff development workshops

3. Inviting teachers or consultants from outside the school to hold workshops
4. Attending conferences or workshops held by professional organizations, publishers, and cultural agencies sponsored by foreign governments
5. Attending college or university classes
6. Attending workshops and seminars sponsored by offices of county superintendents of schools and the California State Department of Education
7. Being involved with the local target language community, including staying with families or others who speak the language as natives
8. Participating in teacher exchange programs
9. Studying and traveling abroad
10. Having access to collections of professional books, tapes, films, and periodicals in local, district, or county libraries

Curriculum Integration

Schools that are serious about the mission of teaching additional languages find ways to integrate the use of foreign languages with other curriculum areas in a mutually enriching fashion. The point to be emphasized is that a second language is a medium for communication. Exactly what is communicated through the medium of language can run the gamut from staging a skit based on a dramatic moment from history or world literature to explaining a mathematics operation or science lesson. Elementary school planners who sometimes find that curriculum requirements exceed the number of hours available for instruction need not choose between teaching a foreign language and other requirements. An option is to cover certain materials in the foreign language—thereby efficiently accomplishing both objectives.

Foreign language teachers and teachers of English as a second language should coordinate their lessons with other teachers. Coordination helps teachers to ensure they have included specific content that reinforces lessons across the curriculum. Correspondingly, teachers of other subjects should take every opportunity to explain foreign language expressions and cultural features in the broad context of their discipline. The ultimate integration of curriculum components with foreign language instruction occurs in immersion-type schools in which the staff teaches all subjects in the target language.

Communication-Oriented Evaluations

The proper guidelines for assessing the outcome of language programs are the overall goal and the major objectives set forth in the curriculum guide. Traditionally, many teachers have been content to evaluate students' mastery of the component language skills, skills that are parts of the language learning process. How many words do the students know? How well can they pronounce and write them? Can students understand written or oral sentences containing those

Schools should integrate the use of foreign languages with other areas of the curriculum in a mutually enriching fashion.

22

words? How well do they understand the grammar of the language? Can students demonstrate this knowledge by analyzing or generating sentences with various specific grammatical structures?

Teachers of languages once assumed that possessing component language skills led directly to proficiency in using the language. But research suggests that while work on structural components may not exclude the possibility of gaining communicative competence, neither does it vigorously promote it. Therefore, the present practice is to test communicative competency directly at various stages of learning. What kinds of messages about what kinds of content are students capable of understanding and producing? When students communicate, what kinds of communicative purposes are they able to fulfill? How fluently and accurately can they fulfill them? Can students read and write (at the appropriate stages) with comparable competency?

Communicative competency should be tested directly at various stages of learning.

Comprehensive testing of students' overall ability to use a language is called proficiency testing. It is an integrated assessment of what students can do when employing the language for communicative ends. This assessment places scores students receive on a scale ranging from zero to native proficiency. Such testing should be done at major points in the learning sequence—at the end of a course or series of courses, entering a new grade level or graduating, or applying for a job requiring a certain language proficiency.

Teachers mainly administer achievement tests, tests designed to assess students' mastery of short-term segments of the learning activity. Those segments may involve such acts as greeting, giving commands, apologizing, or ordering a meal. The acts might involve the use of certain rules of grammar or vocabulary.

However, the total of such evaluations (often called formative evaluations) at frequent points during the learning process does not by itself indicate the students' ability to get along in unrehearsed situations requiring a certain level of general competency in the language. Testing such overall competency at the end of a significant period of learning (often called summative evaluations) is necessary for determining the effectiveness of a communication-based course or program.

The results obtained when individual students have been evaluated provide the major indicator of whether or not the instructional program is working. Several components of the program can be closely examined if objectives are not being reached:

1. Are the objectives realistic?
2. Is the teaching strategy compatible with the objectives?
3. Are the teaching materials compatible with the objectives?
4. Is there adequate district support?
5. Is the staff properly trained in languages and methods?
6. Is the staff maintaining and updating the necessary skill levels?
7. Are the students typical of those making up the average state or national target-language classes?
8. Are there any highly unusual teaching conditions?

The point for teachers and planners to remember is that testing and grading reveal to students the real objectives of instruction. To profess the primacy of communicative outcomes and then measure and grade students' performances in recalling vocabulary, pronouncing and spelling words, doing grammar exercises, and memorizing dialogues and phrases does not convey a consistent message to students. They are unlikely to strive seriously toward the communication objectives under such a testing and grading regime.

Grading ought to reflect all aspects of the instructional process proportionately. In general, if 50 percent of learning time is devoted to achieving proficiency objectives in oral communication, approximately 50 percent of the grade should be based on an evaluation of such activities. If 30 percent of instruction is devoted to reading and writing, 30 percent of the grade should be based on evaluation of such activities. Classroom activities and tests should include elements such as listening comprehension, speaking, reading, writing, conversational skills, cultural skills and knowledge, vocabulary, and accuracy.

However, any system in which credit is given for various separate components of the language learning process (when determining a student's report card grade) is not sufficient by itself to reveal a student's overall competency rating in the language. Increasingly, colleges and employers are requiring an assessment of language competency that goes beyond the traditional transcript grade and number of semesters completed. The student's position on a proficiency or competency scale is becoming recognized as the most significant indicator of the effectiveness of a language program.

Instructional Resources

An effective program of foreign languages uses appropriate instructional resources. By itself the classroom is a somewhat artificial environment in which to learn a foreign language. A student learning to make a request does not have the compelling stimulus of a young traveler getting ready to buy a train ticket in Paris. Nonetheless, well-chosen technology and media aids, realia and printed materials, simulation activities, the students' imagination, and the teacher's creativity can help transform the classroom into a world theater.

Technology and Media Aids

The magic of increasingly sophisticated electronic technology continues to dissolve classroom walls. Native speakers using authentic language in authentic cultural settings can help to sharpen students' comprehension. Large wall projections help to turn the classroom into the Rhine Valley, downtown Tokyo, a family kitchen in Moscow, or a street scene in San Francisco. Videocassettes and tapes allow students to confront teenagers from other countries or cultures in their native language. Computer networks facilitate interaction between students and native speakers. The possibilities for presenting

Instructional resources can help to transform the classroom into a world theater.

and engaging in language interactions in realistic native environments are growing constantly.

Many instructional programs are available for instruction in foreign languages through the use of technology. The quality of those programs varies, and language staffs should review them carefully. Teachers should consider using the California State Department of Education's *Technology in the Curriculum: Foreign Language* when reviewing instructional programs (see Selected References). Most commercial computer programs designed for language instruction can help students practice language components such as structure and vocabulary. In addition, many instructional programs, including those on videocassettes, are designed to help students develop language comprehension skills.

The greatest need is for programs designed to involve students in flexible language interaction. Interaction with technology itself is usually inflexible and limiting. The responses are usually predictable and according to formula. Teachers need to search for materials that students find interesting and that can be used to stimulate students to talk to each other and discuss what is going on.

Realia and Printed Materials

Advanced technology is not the only method teachers can use to introduce students to features of world cultures. For years many teachers have succeeded in simulating characteristics of the target community with books, posters, magazines, newspapers, foods, common objects and implements, visitors, photos, games, stories, and anecdotes. Films, audio recordings, and slides have been used for at least half a century. Many consulates in this country can direct teachers to agencies that distribute foreign language learning and cultural materials. Consulates also can help to establish connections with foreign schools.

Items such as shopping bags, calendars, decals, food packaging labels, maps, train schedules, menus, cookbooks, sport posters, stamps, tickets, and so forth reveal certain dimensions of the culture and provide many possibilities for communicating: What is this used for? How do you use this? What do you think about this? How would you describe this to a friend? Would you enjoy having one of these? Why? Why not? Teachers can encourage students to talk about, hear about, and read and write about such articles.

The direction, objectives, content, instructional approach, and evaluation of language programs often are determined by textbooks. That control is acceptable if a textbook has been found in which all aspects of a language program match their counterparts in the local foreign language curriculum. Such a match is not common, however. Teachers may prefer to leave out sections, rearrange the sequence, use many supplementary materials or content to work toward objectives that differ from those of the author, provide their own audiovisual support, add communicative activities, and plan their own evaluation instruments. As more and better communication-oriented textbooks become available, adapting them to local needs becomes easier.

Sources of Support

An effective foreign language program receives broad support. Teachers of foreign languages need a support system to help students develop their maximum potential. Such a support system includes local school administrators and counselors, district administrators, the board of education, state agencies, and the public. The most important support from those entities is a genuine conviction that languages are of such critical value to California and to individual students that all students are strongly encouraged to learn at least one language in addition to their native language. With such a doctrine in place, other necessary lines of support are likely to follow without great difficulty.

The State Department of Education has identified the need for students to learn foreign languages as a key item on the school reform agenda. Colleges and universities can help by awarding teaching credentials to candidates who are proficient in the target language and well versed in communication-based teaching methods.

The most important support is a genuine conviction that languages are of such critical value to California and to individual students that all students are strongly encouraged to learn at least one language in addition to their native language.

Schools and Districts

At the local level, school district and school administrators are responsible for:

1. Considering alignment of their foreign language improvement efforts with the state's framework and textbook adoption cycle
2. Allocating a fair proportion of available funds for proper staffing of foreign language departments, purchasing learning materials and equipment, and providing staff development
3. Providing a well-qualified curriculum specialist who understands and supports foreign language education
4. Establishing conditions whereby only teachers competent in the languages and in teaching for communication are recruited, hired, assigned, and retained
5. Evaluating foreign language teachers by using criteria primarily based on the attainment of program objectives
6. Informing the governing board about critical foreign language needs

Counselors are responsible for:

1. Recognizing the rapidly increasing career value of studying a foreign language
2. Encouraging all students to begin the study of a second language as early as possible and to continue the study as long as possible
3. Consulting with the language staff about the placement of students in language classes
4. Advising students early about high school and college requirements regarding foreign languages

The school board is responsible for:

1. Recognizing the value of providing foreign language opportunities for all students
2. Providing support for expanding foreign language programs until they span all grade levels in the district
3. Establishing programs in uncommonly taught languages, especially those of the Pacific Rim
4. Supporting professional growth by providing incentives such as recognition and financial assistance
5. Ensuring hiring practices that place only qualified teachers in foreign language classrooms
6. Furnishing adequate funding for expanding programs and enrollment and for ensuring reasonable class size
7. Facilitating students' participation in worthwhile learning experiences requiring travel and board approval

Business and Industry

Support for foreign language and international education programs is in the best interest of most businesses. Schools should take the initiative in forming alliances with firms located in the community. Cooperative efforts may lead to results such as:

1. Technical assistance and equipment for classroom use
2. Financial support for scholarships, language camps and field days, and exchange-student programs
3. Internships for foreign language and other language students
4. Public awareness campaigns to advocate additional study of foreign languages and cultures
5. Contacts with agencies and people in other countries
6. Speakers to motivate and inform language students
7. Support from governing boards and politicians for language education

Local Communities

Many communities have resources valuable to language students and teachers. Native speakers of the target language often volunteer to help in the classroom. They coach students, make conversation, give talks, lead and stimulate small-group activities, and accompany classes on field trips.

Members of the community, especially parents, can provide support for language programs. Most parents are eager to help once they are informed how they can help. In addition to providing direct assistance, many parents may be willing to motivate others to support the language program. However, teachers must reach out to the community to gain this support.

Teachers should consider encouraging members of the community to:

1. Serve as members of language booster groups.
2. Help teachers prepare instructional materials.

3. Serve as classroom aides.
4. Sponsor and help with cocurricular language activities.
5. Host visitors and exchange students from other countries.
6. Lobby elected officials on behalf of language programs.
7. Serve on school-organized task forces formed to make recommendations about language training.
8. Help students with homework assignments.
9. Persuade community organizations and service clubs to sponsor, support, or publicize projects benefiting foreign language education.
10. Serve as resources for authentic target-language experiences.

VI. Instruction in English as a Second Language

Instruction in English as a second language has distinctive planning requirements. These requirements concern the following areas:

- Needs of instructional programs
- Goals of instructional programs
- Nature of instruction
- Structure of the program
- The role of teachers, administrators, governing boards, and local communities

INSTRUCTION IN ENGLISH AS A SECOND LANGUAGE REQUIRES flexibility. The students' cultural backgrounds vary widely, as do their ages and grade levels, fluency in native languages, and ability to adjust to American society.

In spite of such a varied student population, classes in English as a second language must provide appropriate and effective instruction in English to all students. Those classes must also provide content instruction that meshes with the overall school curriculum and, simultaneously, respects the students' primary language. The process of adapting to the culture of the English-speaking majority often reduces the self-confidence and self-esteem of limited-English-proficient students. Those students feel uncomfortable and inadequate within an English-only setting. Limited-English-proficient students need help to develop pride and confidence in their unique abilities in both their native language and in English.

Educators planning effective instruction in English as a second language should be familiar with the professional literature about foreign language instruction. They must also study the literature about teaching English to speakers of other languages, especially in schools in the United States (see Selected References). Instruction in English as a second language has distinctive planning requirements. These

In spite of a varied student population, classes in English as a second language must provide appropriate and effective instruction in English to all students.

requirements concern needs, goals, nature of instruction, and the structure of the program. Information about each area follows.

Needs of Instructional Programs

Educators should consider the following needs when planning instructional programs in English as a second language:

1. California and the nation need *all* students to be able to function independently and cooperatively, both personally and professionally.
2. The individual student needs to be able to function effectively in the general school curriculum and in an English-speaking society.
3. Instruction in English as a second language needs:
   a. Uniquely prepared teachers
   b. Adequate support from teachers, administrators, governing boards, and local communities
   c. Well-designed, appropriate materials
   d. Articulated learning sequences to ensure continuous progress
   e. Evaluations based on how well students perform in situations requiring the use of English
   f. A reliable proficiency scale and definitions by which learning can be guided and evaluated

Goals of Instructional Programs

Students who successfully complete instruction in English as a second language should be able to:

1. Function well enough in English to be successful in programs designed for native speakers of English.
2. Function successfully in the general school curriculum as appropriate for age, ability, and experience.
3. Demonstrate continuous progress without special instruction in English.
4. Demonstrate improved self-confidence and self-esteem in both an English-speaking environment and in their native-language environment.

Nature of Instruction

Educators should consider the following aspects of instruction in English as a second language. Instruction in English:

1. Is required for those assigned to such instruction and is not an elective
2. Is taught in the surroundings of the target-language culture, in contrast to foreign language instruction
3. Is developmental in nature, not remedial
4. Is not the same as instruction in English as a foreign language, which is taught in a non-English-speaking society to relatively homogeneous groups of learners

5. Is flexible enough to meet widely varying student needs
6. Is a long-term process, usually requiring three to five years for students to reach adequate proficiency in English
7. In the beginning stages of instruction, focuses primarily on life skills of immediate concern and reflects a strong sense of urgency for students to learn to function in school and in society as rapidly as possible
8. At later stages of instruction, focuses on subjects in the school's core curriculum, including advanced literacy for the different levels of proficiency of English
9. Includes coordinated, articulated instruction in the areas of listening, speaking, reading, and writing and incorporates the subskills of grammar, vocabulary, and phonetics
10. Is carefully integrated and coordinated with the core curriculum of the school
11. Features planned cocurricular and extracurricular experiences facilitating positive student interaction with native speakers of English
12. Often includes students who must be taught basic learning and literacy skills (how to listen, speak, read, and write)
13. Features careful assessments of students before they are assigned to appropriate classes within the system and levels within the class until they progress beyond classes in English as a second language
14. Provides for continuing assessment of progress and follow-up services

Program Structure

Goals and objectives of instruction in English as a second language should be explicit and relate directly to what students should be able to accomplish through the use of English. The objectives should state what skills and knowledge students should be able to demonstrate in the curriculum subjects.

Instructional approaches or methods should involve the students in learning to perform those behaviors described in the goals and objectives. No one approach is best for all teachers and students. Teachers know and understand that theories and methods of language acquisition are eclectic. They understand the nature of language, particularly English, and the American culture. They demonstrate proficiency in spoken and written English at a level commensurate with their role as language models. They have had the experience of learning another language and have an understanding of another cultural system. And they use a variety of approaches appropriate to students' language levels, academic proficiency, and communicative needs.

Instruction in English as a second language should be available at all levels, kindergarten through grade twelve, with instruction appropriate to students' ages, degree of literacy, and previous (and current) academic experience. Instruction should also be appropriate

Instruction in English as a second language should be available at all levels, kindergarten through grade twelve.

to the extent of current instruction in students' primary language, the cultural adjustment made by students, and students' English proficiency levels. Other instructional services involving language and content should also be considered when planning instruction in English as a second language.

Teachers must be qualified, well-prepared, and properly credentialed to do the following:

1. Teach English to nonnative speakers.
2. Work with students who represent a variety of native languages, cultural values, attitudes toward education, previous educational experiences, difficulties with the culture, and so forth.
3. Incorporate content from a variety of subjects—science, mathematics, social studies, and so forth—in classes in English as a second language.
4. In many cases teach beginning learning and literacy skills.
5. Handle many sensitive counseling/guidance responsibilities and home-school relationships.
6. Work with instructional aides.

Evaluation in English as a second language instruction should measure the following:

1. Entry-level skills—to ensure proper placement in the school and in English instruction
2. Proficiency gains in the ability to communicate in English
3. Skills and knowledge gained in the school subjects included in the students' program
4. Willingness of students to use English in the school and community
5. Students' success after leaving regular classes in English as a second language
6. Effectiveness of the instructional process itself: its objectives, content, materials, methods, staff assignments, placement procedures, and support

Resources used in instruction in English as a second language should include the following:

1. Printed materials, especially in the early stages of instruction, that correspond to students' ages and English proficiency levels and contain instructional strategies for teaching English as a second language
2. Authentic textbooks, selected and presented with appropriate instructional strategies
3. Literature-based content materials
4. Technology such as videocassettes, films, recordings, and computers to provide a variety of language experiences
5. Members of the community who provide or sponsor teachers' aides, social group activities, appropriate jobs, or work experiences

6. Cooperation of the school in pairing nonnative speakers with native speakers of English
7. Planned cocurricular activities in which interaction in English is stressed
8. Staff development in acquiring sensitivity to and appropriate instructional techniques for students of English as a second language
9. Planned linkage between the content of English classes and regular classes
10. Cooperation between foreign language teachers and teachers of English as a second language in areas such as proficiency testing, student pairing, instructional techniques, and so forth

Support for programs in English as a second language must come from:

1. A community whose members understand and back the special efforts required of teachers of English as a second language to encourage students to develop their full potential
2. Administrators and members of governing boards who recognize the special needs and importance of instruction in English as a second language, adequately fund such instruction, search for and assign well-qualified teachers, and grant credit for work that meets the districts' graduation requirements in English
3. Teachers of other subjects who recognize the special needs of limited-English-proficient students and adjust their teaching accordingly

Role of Teachers, Administrators, Governing Boards, and Local Communities

Helping students actively master a variety of languages is a central goal of California's educational reform movement. To help teachers achieve that goal, the California State Department of Education is recommending and many schools throughout California are adopting a qualitatively new approach—communication-based language instruction. However, additional steps need to be taken by forward-looking teachers, school administrators, school boards, and friends of education. These essential initiatives include providing:

1. *A volume and variety of classes.* Schools must provide additional classes in English as a second language and encourage more students to enroll in them.
2. *Course offerings.* Students must be given the opportunity to begin the study of English as a second language whenever they enter school.
3. *Articulation of the program.* A standard description of what constitutes successive levels of language competency must be written so that students experience a smooth transition between schools and school levels.

Teachers, administrators, and members of school boards and local communities must realize the importance of the English language to new immigrants.

33

4. *Methods of evaluation.* Assessment of students' language proficiencies must be based on how well they can actually communicate in unrehearsed encounters, oral or written.
5. *Professional teachers.* Only teachers who are proficient in the target language and are able to develop communicative competencies in students should be assigned to teach classes in English as a second language. School districts should support regular staff development for current teachers.
6. *Sufficient number of teachers.* Teacher education institutions should recruit and prepare more teachers of English as a second language.
7. *Communication-based materials.* The California State Department of Education and school districts in California should approve or adopt only communiciation-based textbooks for use in classes in English as a second language.

VII. Criteria for Evaluating Instructional Materials

IF A REFORM-MINDED SCHOOL DISTRICT WERE TO IMPLEMENT every recommendation included in this framework but overlook the issue of appropriate instructional materials, the prospects for improvement in its foreign language program would be severely compromised.

Research confirms that textbooks and other instructional materials have a pervasive influence on the quality of the classroom experience. Textbooks that habitually treat the target language as a grammatical jigsaw puzzle to be assembled piece by piece by students undermine the purpose of a communication-based program, which is to present languages as a means of communicating and understanding the historically rich cultures from which they come.

The evaluation criteria included in this chapter are designed to assist publishers in developing the kind of instructional materials that support the purposes of this framework.[1] These criteria should serve as standards for the statewide adoption of instructional materials in kindergarten through grade eight. They also can be used as guidelines in preparing and reviewing materials for grades nine through twelve.

Textbooks should present languages as a means of communicating and understanding the historically rich cultures from which they come.

Basic Guidelines

The basic guidelines to be used in considering textbooks and other instructional materials follow:

1. Textbooks and other instructional materials must reflect and support the communication-based goals and objectives recommended in this framework.

---

[1] In addition, publishers should note the relevant portions of the California *Education Code* and the requirements for evaluating instructional materials included in *Standards for Evaluation of Instructional Materials with Respect to Social Content* (see Selected References).

2. Cumulatively, learning objectives in a given set of materials should cover the main concepts found in standard proficiency and competency scales.
3. The presentation of new language content/vocabulary should correspond generally to the guidelines described in the *Model Curriculum Standards* (see Selected References). Content should be articulated from level to level and allow for entry at various levels without undue difficulty.
4. Explanations of language structure or other grammatical components should be subordinated to communicative activities.
5. Evaluation should be designed to assess communicative proficiency.
6. Instructional materials should include facsimiles of items from the target language. The facsimiles, which should provide students with a sense of the cultural milieu, might include advertisements, significant documents, newspaper articles, poetry, excerpts from diaries, or other examples of the literature. These materials should be suitable and designed to provoke the interest of students in various age groups, initiate discussions, or inform students about the target society.
7. The materials should give an accurate view of present-day life in the culture being studied as well as a sense of its history and roots.
8. Language samples presented in the materials should use authentic speech patterns and expressions from the target culture. Cultural features should be integrated throughout the materials and serve as a natural dimension of the total communicative process and as a spur to heightened global awareness.
9. The target language is not what is found sandwiched between the covers of a single hefty textbook but rather, a living, dynamic entity with inexhaustible possibilities for communication. Publishers should consider adopting formats (other than the standard hardbound textbook) that reinforce the dynamism of language.

Organization of Materials

The instructional materials should have the following characteristics:

1. An organizational structure for textbooks that includes an introduction, table of contents, and English/foreign language and foreign language/English glossary (except in the case of textbooks used in classes for English as a second language)
2. An introduction to the student's edition that includes a statement about the point of view and goals and objectives of the content as well as information about the organizational structure

36

3. Units, chapters, and lessons organized around communication objectives that state what students will be able to accomplish when they have successfully completed a segment
4. A format in which lessons are organized so that they follow the learning sequence of introduction, presentation, guided practice, application, and evaluation
5. Alignment of all elements of the instructional materials, such as the students' materials, teacher's manual, audiovisual materials, and software, into an integrated, purposeful whole
6. A variety of intellectually stimulating communication activities that are appropriate for use by students with a wide range of abilities and that allow for creative responses and interpretations
7. Maximum reliance on the target language when giving directions and explanations
8. The introduction of new vocabulary in the context of specific content areas and, once introduced, the recycling of high-frequency, useful language throughout the textbook and in succeeding textbooks
9. Language structures that are learned through instruction in listening, speaking, reading, and writing for communication
10. Reading passages that are inherently interesting and not translated (A glossary, when deemed necessary, should not appear on the same page as the text.)

Teachers' Manuals and Reference Materials

The teachers' manuals and reference materials should include:

1. An overview or summary or both for each unit, including goals and objectives clearly stated in communication terms, and examples of creative language application activities
2. A variety of evaluation components that are closely correlated with the students' textbooks
3. Suggestions for teaching students of varying abilities and for presenting the material through individual as well as group activities
4. Suggestions for integrating other curriculum areas with the target language
5. A variety of ways to extend students' learning beyond the textbook and classroom, including a bibliography of professional references and resources
6. Suggestions for extending the program by involving parents and members of the community

Assessment and Evaluation

The assessment and evaluation features of the material should include:

1. A focus on the students' abilities to comprehend and manipulate the language in communicative contexts (The effort

should be directed toward evaluating the students' capacity to understand and be understood in communicative encounters.)

2. Short-term assessment as well as periodic broader language summative evaluations
3. Evaluation of proficiency in all communicative modes—listening, speaking, reading, and writing—with attention paid to the cultural appropriateness of students' responses
4. Suggestions for evaluating the effectiveness of the language program

Instructional Media

The instructional media for the program must be of high technical quality, cross-referenced to the teacher's materials, and designed to extend classroom activities. The media should include:

1. Visual nonprint materials such as films, videotapes, filmstrips, charts, maps, and reproductions. Visual nonprint materials must be (a) objective, current, appropriate, and culturally authentic; (b) responsive to the needs and comprehension of students at a given age and grade level; and (c) likely to stimulate a reaction.
2. Materials designed for listening, such as records and tapes. This material must also be (a) appropriate in content and length for students; (b) clearly and appropriately narrated in a pitch that does not distract from or obscure the message being conveyed; and (c) recorded in the standard target language.
3. Technology-related materials, such as instructional television, computer software, or interactive videocassette programs, should be integrally related to other instructional materials and be suitable for use as a replacement or supplement for textbooks. Electronic media must also (a) meet the standards for exemplary software described in *Guidelines for Educational Software in California Schools* (see Selected References); (b) stimulate students to communicate with one another; and (c) be available in multiple machine or operating system formats.

Selected References

Academic Preparation in Foreign Language. New York: The College Board, 1986.

"ACTFL Provisional Program Guidelines for Foreign Language Teacher Education," *Foreign Language Annals,* Vol. 21 (February, 1988), 71—82.

American Council on the Teaching of Foreign Languages Proficiency Guidelines. Yonkers, N.Y.: American Council on the Teaching of Foreign Languages, 1986. (Copies available from the Council, 6 Executive Blvd., Upper Level, Yonkers, NY 10701; telephone 914-478-2011)

Baker, Charlotte, and Robin Battison. *Sign Language and the Deaf Community: Essays in Honor of William Stokoe.* Silver Spring, Md.: National Association of the Deaf, 1981.

Baldegger, Markus, and Martin Mueller. *Kontaktschwelle Deutsch als Fremdsprache.* New York: Langenscheidt, 1980.

Boyer, Ernest. *High School: Report on Secondary Education in America.* New York: Harper and Row, Publishers, 1983.

California 2000: A People in Transition. Sacramento: Assembly Office of Research, 1986.

Cokely, Dennis, and Charlotte Baker. *American Sign Language: A Teacher's Resource Text on Curriculum, Methods, and Evaluation.* Silver Spring, Md.: T.J. Publishers, Inc., 1980.

Defining and Developing Proficiency. Edited by Michael J. Canale and Heidi Byrnes. Lincolnwood, Ill.: National Textbook Co., 1986.

Educating Americans for Tomorrow's World: State Initiatives in International Education, Richmond, Va.: National Governors' Association, 1987.

Foreign Language Proficiency in the Classroom and Beyond. Edited by Charles J. James. Lincolnwood, Ill.: National Textbook Co., 1985.

Gannon, Jack. *Deaf Heritage: A Narrative History of Deaf America.* Silver Spring, Md.: National Association of the Deaf, 1981.

Goodman, Kenneth. *What's Whole in Whole Language?* Portsmouth, N.H.: Heinemann Educational Books, Inc., 1986.

Guidelines for Educational Software in California Schools. Sacramento: California State Department of Education, 1985.

Handbook for Planning an Effective Foreign Language Program. Sacramento: California State Department of Education, 1985.

Interactive Language Teaching. Edited by Wilga M. Rivers. New York: Cambridge University Press, 1987.

Jacobs, Leo M. *A Deaf Adult Speaks Out* (Second revised edition). Washington, D.C.: Gallaudet University Press, 1981.

Kelly, Louis G. *Twenty-Five Centuries of Language Teaching.* Rowley, Mass.: Newbury House Publishers, 1969.

Klima, Edward S., and Ursula Bellugi. *The Signs of Language.* Cambridge, Mass.: Harvard University Press, 1979.

Larsen-Freeman, Diane. *Techniques and Principles in Language Teaching.* New York: Oxford University Press, Inc., 1986.

Looking to California's Pacific Neighborhood. Sacramento: California Postsecondary Education Commission, 1987.

Lowe, Pardee, Jr. "Proficiency-Based Curriculum Design: Principles Derived from Government Experience," *Die Unterrichtspraxis,* Vol. 18 (Fall, 1985), 233—45.

Methods That Work. Edited by John W. Oller, Jr., and Patricia Richard-Amato. New York: Newbury House Publishers, 1983.

Model Curriculum Standards, Grades Nine Through Twelve. Sacramento: California State Department of Education, 1985.

The Natural Approach: Language Acquisition in the Classroom. Edited by Stephen D. Krashen and Tracy D. Terrell. Hayward, Calif.: Alemany Press, Inc., 1983.

Omaggio, Alice C. *Teaching Language in Context: Proficiency-Oriented Instruction.* Boston: Heinle and Heinle Publishers, Inc., 1986.

Practical Ideas for Teaching Writing as a Process. Sacramento: California State Department of Education, 1987.

Sign and Culture: A Reader for Students of America Sign Language. Edited by William C. Stokoe. Silver Spring, Md.: Linstok Press, Inc., 1980.

Smith, Frank. *Insult to Intelligence: The Bureaucratic Invasion of Our Classrooms* (Revised edition). Portsmouth, N.H.: Heinemann Educational Books, Inc., 1988.

Smith, Frank. *Reading Without Nonsense* (Second edition). New York: Columbia University Teachers College Press, 1985.

Standards for Evaluation of Instructional Materials with Respect to Social Content. Sacramento: California State Department of Education, 1986.

Statement on Competencies in Languages Other Than English Expected of Entering Freshmen: Phase I-French, German, Spanish. Sacramento: The Academic Senates of the California Community Colleges, The California State University, and the University of California, 1986.

Teaching for Proficiency: The Organizing Principle. Edited by Theodore V. Higgs. Lincolnwood, Ill.: National Textbook Co., 1984.

Technology in the Curriculum: Foreign Language. Sacramento: California State Department of Education, 1987.

Terrell, Tracy David. "Recent Trends in Research and Practice: Teaching Spanish," *Hispania,* Vol. 69 (March, 1986), n.p.

Appendix A

Comparison of Features in Effective and Less Effective Foreign Language Programs

The Exemplary District	The Less Effective District
1. Demonstrates a commitment of support for foreign languages, English as a second language, and other languages	1. Shows indifference toward foreign languages, English as a second language, and other languages
2. Supports articulated programs in the languages for students in kindergarten through grade twelve	2. Provides for only one or two years of instruction
3. Establishes second-language programs for all students	3. Offers courses for college preparatory or severely limited-English-proficient students only
4. Offers a variety of foreign languages	4. Offers only one or two foreign languages
5. Offers specific and regular in-service staff development for language teachers	5. Provides little or no in-service teacher education
6. Hires teachers who are appropriately credentialed and have demonstrated proficiency in the language and skill in applying the appropriate methodologies	6. Hires credentialed teachers without regard to demonstrated language skills
7. Develops a curriculum guide that: a. Has a communication-based focus b. Integrates a study of language with culture c. Integrates/collaborates with other subject areas	7. Develops a curriculum guide that is grammar-based and driven by the choice of textbooks
8. Facilitates the use of the community as a resource	8. Overlooks the use of the community as a resource
9. Establishes equitable funding for language programs	9. Provides insufficient funding
10. Provides communication-based materials	10. Provides grammar-based textbooks
11. Establishes a student/teacher ratio that facilitates communicative activities	11. Permits class sizes that are not conducive to communication-based instruction
12. Establishes a mechanism for appropriate student placement	12. Has inadequate placement procedures

Exemplary Instruction	Less Effective Instruction
1. Is student centered	1. Is teacher centered
2. Meets expectations and needs of students	2. Follows a set curriculum without regard to students' needs
3. Features much communicative activity	3. Focuses on drill and grammatical explanations
4. Provides for language comprehension before production is required	4. Often features student production of language before students can comprehend the language involved
5. Features a variety of activities, well-paced throughout instruction time	5. Features only one or two activities per instructional time period
6. Provides for grouping students in a variety of ways to maximize interaction	6. Focuses on whole-group activities
7. Includes physical movement during communicative interaction	7. Takes place where students must be quiet and passive and are not permitted to move around
8. Presents the target language through content in realistic contexts	8. Emphasizes studying about the target language and its mechanics
9. Uses the target language as the instructional medium	9. Uses the students' native language as the instructional medium (an undesirable practice, except in the case of classes in native-language development)
10. Uses a variety of materials, including those presented through the use of technology	10. Uses the textbook only
11. Guides students to experience and enjoy the best examples of the literature in the language	11. Presents literature as a translation exercise
12. Provides activities that encourage divergent thinking and negotiation	12. Emphasizes only one correct answer
13. Is supportive and nonthreatening in an environment conducive to employing the language	13. Emphasizes constant correction
14. Encourages students to also use the language outside the classroom	14. Leads students to view the language only as an academic subject
15. Includes content and activities for increasing students' awareness of cross-cultural, international, and global considerations	15. Adheres mainly to matters of language and structure rather than stressing the value of vital content
16. Takes place daily for at least one instructional hour	16. Takes place only a few days a week or month for very short periods of time
17. Focuses evaluation on students' overall abilities to use the target language for communication	17. Focuses evaluation on short-term mastery of discrete elements of the language

The Exemplary Student

1. Communicates effectively and with appropriate cultural sensitivity in at least one language in addition to his or her native language

2. Continues study of the language and develops higher levels of proficiency

3. Wants to learn additional languages

4. Seeks opportunities to participate in language and cultural activities and engages in life-long learning

5. Seeks opportunities to use the language in the community

6. Has new insights into his or her native language

7. Feels comfortable in cross-cultural settings

8. Has enhanced thinking and problem-solving skills

9. Uses language readily as a tool for getting to know people from other cultures

10. Is motivated to continue finding out about people, cultures, history, literature, art, music, and so forth connected with the target language

11. Broadens language and cultural knowledge through international travel and study

12. Gains enhanced prestige and employability

13. Has increased awareness of other people and cultures, global issues, and world affairs

Appendix B

Comparison of Features in Communication-Based Activities and Manipulative Activities

In communication-based instruction information is conveyed or messages are exchanged naturally during the learning process. Students participating in communication-based activities have a purpose for communicating and attach personal significance to the content.

Communication-Based Activity	Manipulative Activity
Beginning students sit in pairs, back to back, and look at similar pictures. They describe and ask questions until they can identify the differences among the pictures.	Beginning students memorize ten words. As the teacher dictates, the students write the sentences containing the memorized words.
After donning an unusual variety of clothing provided by the teacher, beginning students narrate a fashion show. Groups then select the model most appropriately dressed for a date, a sporting event, school, and so forth.	The teacher points to an article of clothing on a chart and asks what it is and what color it is. Individual students respond; the teacher gives the correct response; the entire class repeats the correct response.
Intermediate students create their own written questionnaire to elicit personal information (address, telephone number, and likes and dislikes). The questionnaires are given to other students at random who complete them. Questionnaires are then read aloud by the originator or posted for students to read and to guess who the person is.	Students are given a printed questionnaire with ten questions and 20 possible answers. Students copy a plausible answer in the blank after each question.
Intermediate students observe several short presentations about biological medicine. (The computer and videocassette presentations in the target language have been prepared in cooperation with the subject-matter teachers.) Students take notes and then meet in groups to compare and adjust their notes before writing a report.	Students read a two-page passage about the agricultural production of Germany. They answer 25 questions about the passage. The questions are in the order in which the information is presented in the passage.
Advanced learners in groups discuss a news article with a unique cultural twist. The teacher has chosen the article from a target-language newspaper. The students decide on one group opinion about the significance or puzzling nature of the article. Leaders report the group opinion; other students may ask questions or offer other opinions.	The teacher shows slides about a country in which the target language is spoken. Students ask questions about the content of the slides. The teacher then gives a true-false quiz in English on the geography and culture depicted in the slides.
Advanced students watch a videocassette or short film of people reacting to various situations in the culture in which the target language is spoken. They are asked to tell or write three or four things that they would have done if they had been present. Other students may ask why a student gave a particular response.	Students are given ten sentences in the present tense. They are to combine them into five conditional sentences in the past tense.

Competency Levels

	Novice	Intermediate	Advanced	Superior	Distinguished
Listening	Understands learned material at an elementary level	Understands routine speech and conversations	Understands main ideas and details of many kinds of presentations	Understands all standard speech, including idioms and subtleties	Understands all forms and styles of speech
Reading	Recognizes alphabet and understands learned written material	Understands main ideas, facts, and narratives in textbooks dealing with everyday matters	Understands simple stories, news, letters, and technical textbooks of a general nature	Reads prose, literature, and so forth on a great variety of topics at normal speed	Reads any written material and understands content, intent, cultural references, and so forth
Conversation	Communicates learned material at an elementary level	Participates in basic communication tasks; combines and recombines basic speech elements	Maintains extended conversations; satisfies work and school needs; handles unforeseen problems	Communicates in most formal and informal situations, including abstract matters; can hypothesize and so forth	Communicates on a professional level; can tailor speech to audience; can negotiate, persuade, interpret, and so forth
Writing	Can copy, transcribe, and write learned material	Writes short messages and simple letters; takes notes; writes simple summaries	Writes narratives, descriptions, business correspondence, resumes, and summaries	Expresses self in formal and informal writing; does research papers; writes on professional topics	Writes with precision; can represent a point of view; tailors writing to audience
Culture	Aware of stereotypes; handles cultural dimensions of everyday activities	Perceives cultural differences and recognizes points of misunderstanding; handles more complex situations	Demonstrates important cultural behaviors; knows how misunderstandings arise; handles personal relationships and historical references	Handles most native customs, values, and attitudes in most social and professional situations	Near-native proficiency in sensitivity to values, beliefs, geographical differences, and historical conditioning
Content/ Vocabulary	Understands 800 to 1,600 words; uses 300 to 600 words; frequently encounters basic everyday topics	Understands 1,000 to 3,000 words; uses 600 to 1,000 words; frequently encounters general topics	Understands 2,400 to 4,500 words; uses 1,200 to 2,000 words; expands topics to business, politics, and social arrangements	Understands 3,500 to 6,000 words; uses 2,000 to 3,000 words; expands topics to more abstract areas of feeling, emotions, personality, and so forth	Near-native ability in topics and vocabulary handled
Accuracy	Accuracy constitutes the degree of control students have over such aspects as grammar, word choice, cultural appropriateness, graphics, comprehension, and so forth. Accuracy becomes most crucial at any level when errors result in miscommunication. Specific accuracy concerns for each stage of competency development can be found in other publications.				
Competency	Competency is the degree of skill in using all components as integrated acts of communication.				

Note: Material contained in this chart was adapted from *Statement on Competencies in Languages Other Than English Expected of Entering Freshmen: Phase I—French, German, Spanish.* Sacramento: The Academic Senates of the California Community Colleges, The California State University, and the University of California, 1986.

Publications Available from the
Department of Education

This publication is one of over 650 that are available from the California State Department of Education. Some of the more recent publications or those most widely used are the following:

ISBN	Title (Date of publication)	Price
0-801		14.00
0-80		14.00
0-80		8.00
0-80		3.50
0-80		
		5.00
0-80		6.75
0-80		
0-80		3.00
		3.00
0-80		
0-80		5.50
		3.50
0-80		
		3.00
0-80		2.00
0-80		2.50
0-80		2.00
		6.00
0-80	ng	
		6.00
0-80		3.25
0-80		6.00
0-8	lish	4.50
	an,	
0-8		4.00
	blic	
		6.00

Or

Ple N) for each
title o

Re hase orders
witho . Sales tax
shoul

A complete list of publications available from the Department, including apprenticeship instructional materials, may be obtained by writing to the address listed above or by calling (916) 445-1260.

F88-543 (Second printing) (03-0348) 79716-300 7-89 15M